Children's Illustrators

Robert McCloskey

Jill C. Wheeler
ABDO Publishing Company

visit us at
www.abdopub.com

Published by ABDO Publishing Company, 4940 Viking Drive, Edina, Minnesota 55435.
Copyright © 2005 by Abdo Consulting Group, Inc. International copyrights reserved in all
countries. No part of this book may be reproduced in any form without written permission from
the publisher. The Checkerboard Library™ is a trademark and logo of ABDO Publishing
Company.

Printed in the United States.

Cover Photo: AP/Wide World
Interior Photos: AP/Wide World pp. 14, 23; Corbis pp. 9, 11, 13; Fotosearch p. 21; Getty p. 7;
Kerlan Collection, University of Minnesota Libraries pp. 5, 17, 19

Series Coordinator: Jennifer R. Krueger
Editors: Kate A. Conley, Kristin Van Cleaf
Art Direction: Neil Klinepier

Library of Congress Cataloging-in-Publication Data

Wheeler, Jill C., 1964-
    Robert McCloskey / Jill C. Wheeler.
        p. cm. -- (Children's illustrators)
    Includes bibliographical references and index.
    ISBN 1-59197-719-3
    1. McCloskey, Robert, 1914---Juvenile literature. 2. Illustrators--United States--Biography-
-Juvenile literature. I. Title. II. Series.

NC975.5.M353W49 2004
741.6'42'092--dc22

                                                                          2004046119

Contents

Enjoyable Art 4

Boyhood Hobbies 6

Draw What You Know 8

Sketching Ducks.. 12

A Story Takes Shape 14

A Boy Named Homer 16

Life in Maine 18

The Importance of Art................................ 20

Glossary 22

Web Sites 23

Index... 24

Enjoyable Art

Robert McCloskey never planned to become an author and illustrator of children's books. He started out dreaming of becoming a musician or an inventor. Then, he began painting. He designed artwork for other people's projects. And, he created works of art for public buildings.

Though he had many talents, McCloskey was most successful as a children's book illustrator. He is best known for writing and illustrating *Make Way for Ducklings*. This book has sold more than 2 million copies! It is now a classic in children's literature.

Robert McCloskey's books have delighted readers for more than 60 years. Throughout his career, he received many cards and letters from children, librarians, and parents. They wanted him to know how much they enjoyed his books. Today, his detailed artwork and sense of humor still hold the attention of young readers around the world.

McCloskey believed he saw the world a little differently than most people. He liked to joke that he had one foot on reality and the other on a banana peel.

Boyhood Hobbies

John Robert McCloskey was born on September 15, 1914, in Hamilton, Ohio. His parents were Howard and Mable McCloskey. Robert's parents encouraged him to develop hobbies, and he had many of them.

His first love was music. He played the piano, harmonica, drums, and **oboe**. He thought about becoming a professional musician when he grew up.

Then Robert began collecting electric motors, old clocks, and pieces of wire. With these parts, he invented his own mechanical wonders. He built trains and cranes. He even made his family's Christmas trees **rotate**!

Robert dreamed of being an inventor until he discovered art in high school. He drew pictures for his school yearbook and newspaper. He also held an after-school job with the Young Men's Christian Association (YMCA). There, Robert taught soap carving.

Robert also worked with wood. When he was a senior in high school, he made a **woodcut** engraving and entered it in a contest sponsored by Scholastic Publishing. It won first place! The prize was a four-year **scholarship** to the Vesper George School of Art in Boston, Massachusetts.

McCloskey loved to play the harmonica. He even had an after-school job teaching other kids how to play.

Draw What You Know

McCloskey attended the Vesper George School of Art from 1932 to 1936. In the summers, he brought his love of art to a YMCA camp back in Ohio. There, he carved bigger and bigger pieces. He even carved **totem poles** from tree trunks!

McCloskey's carving talent landed him a job in 1934. He was hired to create more than 20 **bas-reliefs** in stone. They would decorate a public building in Hamilton, Ohio.

This project inspired McCloskey. When he returned to his studies in Boston, he decided he was going to create great art. To him, that meant art based on stories and legends. He worked with images from Greek and Chinese mythology. He made elaborate, dramatic **woodcuts**.

After McCloskey graduated from art school, he moved to New York City to study at the National Academy of Design. He spent two years at the academy. While there, he received honors such as the President's Award. McCloskey then tried to sell some of his work.

Bas-relief sculptures, such as this one of Saint Peter, project slightly from their surrounding material.

McCloskey soon realized that he could not make a lot of money selling his paintings. So, he worked for a while as a **commercial artist**. McCloskey did not enjoy the job, however, and soon quit. He had another idea for his art.

McCloskey showed his **portfolio** to a children's book editor named May Massee. She worked for Viking Press in New York City. Massee could tell that McCloskey had talent. But, she suggested that he draw things he knew more about.

McCloskey took this advice home with him in 1938. He had decided to move back to Ohio. There he added to his portfolio. He drew pictures of what he saw every day.

The new drawings helped McCloskey land another job. He and another artist were hired to create a **mural** for the Lever Brothers offices in Cambridge, Massachusetts. The mural was to feature famous people from Boston.

On the strength of this work, McCloskey won an art prize called the British Prix de Rome in 1939. It included money to pay for studies in Europe. But that year **World War II** began, and it was unsafe to travel in Europe. The war prevented McCloskey from accepting the prize for another ten years.

Opposite Page: *Traveling in Europe during World War II was unsafe. This London railway station was damaged in 1942.*

Sketching Ducks

McCloskey could not study art in Europe. He had other projects to keep him busy, however. He had been writing and illustrating a book about a boy named Lentil.

Lentil cannot whistle or sing. Instead, he learns to play the harmonica. This skill helps him save the day in his small Ohio town. When creating his story, McCloskey followed May Massee's advice. He drew pictures of a midwestern childhood, something he knew best.

McCloskey took his book to Massee. She liked it, and Viking Press published it in 1940. *Lentil* was popular with both readers and critics.

McCloskey had one children's book to his credit. Now, he wanted to use the Boston Public Garden as a setting for a book. He had been thinking about it since studying in Boston in the 1930s.

The Public Garden was home to several families of ducks. McCloskey had heard a story about how the ducks

McCloskey studied the ducks in the Boston Public Garden. There, he discovered the famous Swan Boats, which also appear in Make Way for Ducklings.

once stopped traffic to cross a street. He began to sketch out a story about the ducks and their adventures.

McCloskey showed his early sketches for the duck story to Massee. She agreed it would make a good book. However, she suggested that he learn more about ducks before finishing the sketches.

A Story Takes Shape

McCloskey needed to learn all he could for his sketches. So, he purchased some ducks. He brought them home to his apartment.

McCloskey crawled around on his hands and knees, following the waddling, quacking ducks. He watched how they moved. He watched them splash around in the bathtub. He sketched them from many different angles.

McCloskey was impressed with the duck families that proudly walked around Boston.

McCloskey also worked on the story. It was about Mr. and Mrs. Mallard. They were two ducks looking for a safe place to raise their family in Boston.

Viking agreed to publish the book. McCloskey went to work on the final artwork. He wanted to do the illustrations in watercolor. However, Viking's editors said that would cost too much money. So, he settled on pencil drawings.

Before the book was published, McCloskey was married. His new wife, Margaret Durand, was a children's librarian in New York City. In 1941, the newlyweds celebrated when *Make Way for Ducklings* was finally published.

Elements of Art

Tone

Tone is one of the basic parts of art. It is the level of color in an art piece. Tone can be deep or pale or anywhere in between.

McCloskey used many tones so the ducks of *Make Way for Ducklings* would look as real as possible. Although the ducks were drawn only in the color of pencil, the tone is deep in some places and shallow in others.

In some of his later books, McCloskey used color. The illustrations in *Blueberries for Sal* have a deep tone. They are the color of blueberries!

A Boy Named Homer

Make Way for Ducklings was a success. In 1942, it won the **Caldecott Medal**. That same year, McCloskey joined the army to help in the war effort. He became a sergeant and was stationed in Alabama. He designed equipment that helped the army train soldiers to do their jobs.

After his service, McCloskey continued to draw and write about what he knew. He created a character named Homer Price. Homer is a midwestern boy who gets himself into lots of trouble. But, he always manages to get out of it. *Homer Price* was published in 1943.

McCloskey was also working on building a family. He and his wife had a daughter named Sarah in 1945. They had a second daughter, Jane, in 1948.

After Jane's birth, McCloskey was finally able to collect his British Prix de Rome prize. The family spent a year in Italy. While there, McCloskey studied **mosaic** techniques in glass and marble.

McCloskey enjoyed entertaining Jane (left) and Sarah with his drawings.

Life in Maine

The McCloskey family returned to the United States after their year in Italy. They lived on an island off the coast of Maine. Maine quickly became another source of book ideas for McCloskey. The first was *Blueberries for Sal*.

Blueberries for Sal is the story of a mother and child, Sal, who go blueberry picking. Viking published *Blueberries for Sal* in 1948. Unlike *Make Way for Ducklings*, its illustrations were a purple-blue color. It was named a **Caldecott Honor Book** in 1949.

McCloskey's Maine home appeared in three more of his books, including *One Morning in Maine*, *Time of Wonder*, and *Burt Dow: Deep-Water Man*. *One Morning in Maine* was a Caldecott Honor Book. *Time of Wonder* won the Caldecott Medal in 1958. McCloskey was the first person to win the award twice.

McCloskey's daughter Sarah was the model for Sal in Blueberries for Sal.

The Importance of Art

Burt Dow was the last book McCloskey wrote. He only illustrated ten works by other authors. McCloskey admitted he did not produce a lot of books. He once said that it took time for ideas to "bubble out." It also took time for him to research his subjects. He spent years working on each book.

McCloskey took his art seriously. Throughout his career, McCloskey talked about the importance of art. He often said that children should learn to make pictures. He urged teachers to think of art as a basic subject, along with reading and writing.

The importance of McCloskey's art was recognized in 1987. The city of Boston erected a new sculpture in the Boston Public Garden. It was a sculpture of Mrs. Mallard and her ducklings. It was designed to be big enough for children to play on.

Robert McCloskey died on June 30, 2003, in Deer Isle, Maine. He was 88 years old. McCloskey's books have been popular for generations. Today, children, parents, and librarians continue to enjoy his funny stories and timeless illustrations.

A child plays on the sculpture of Mrs. Mallard and her ducklings in the Boston Public Garden.

Glossary

bas-relief - a carving or sculpture that leaves a design that is only slightly raised from the surface.

Caldecott Medal - an award the American Library Association gives to the artist who illustrated the year's best picture book. Runners-up are called Caldecott Honor Books.

commercial artist - an artist who works for businesses.

mosaic - pieces of glass, stone, or other materials that fit together to create a picture.

mural - a picture painted on a wall or ceiling.

oboe - a high-pitched woodwind instrument.

portfolio - a body of work held in one case that displays an artist's talent.

rotate - to turn around a fixed center.

scholarship - a gift of money to help a student pay for instruction.

totem pole - a carved and painted pole that is a symbol of a family or clan in Native American societies.

woodcut - a block of wood that has been carved away to leave a raised design.

World War II - from 1939 to 1945, fought in Europe, Asia, and Africa. Great Britain, France, the United States, the Soviet Union, and their allies were on one side. Germany, Italy, Japan, and their allies were on the other side.

Web Sites

To learn more about Robert McCloskey, visit ABDO Publishing Company on the World Wide Web at **www.abdopub.com**. Web sites about Robert McCloskey are featured on our Book Links page. These links are routinely monitored and updated to provide the most current information available.

The Library of Congress named McCloskey a Living Legend in April 2000.

Index

A

Alabama 16
army service 16

B

Blueberries for Sal 18
Boston, Massachusetts 7, 8, 10, 12, 14, 20
Boston Public Garden 12, 20
British Prix de Rome 10, 16
Burt Dow: Deep-Water Man 18, 20

C

Caldecott Honor Book 18
Caldecott Medal 16, 18
Cambridge, Massachusetts 10
carving 7, 8
commercial art 10

D

Deer Isle, Maine 21

E

Europe 10, 12

F

family 6, 15, 16, 18

H

Hamilton, Ohio 6, 8
Homer Price 16

I

Italy 16, 18

L

Lentil 12
Lever Brothers offices 10

M

Maine 18, 21
Make Way for Ducklings 4, 12, 13, 14, 15, 16, 18, 20
Massee, May 10, 12, 13

N

National Academy of Design 8
New York City, New York 8, 10, 15

O

Ohio 8, 10, 12
One Morning in Maine 18

P

President's Award 8

S

Scholastic Publishing contest 7

T

Time of Wonder 18

V

Vesper George School of Art 7, 8
Viking Press 10, 12, 15, 18

W

World War II 10

Y

Young Men's Christian Association (YMCA) 6, 8